AF415725

Name

Draw a Picture

I Can...

- [ ] use a Capital Letter
  <u>T</u>he cat is big.

- [ ] use spaces

- [ ] sound out words
  d-o-g = dog

- [ ] use a Period .

- [ ] Draw a picture

He is having fun, running under the sun with his new toy gun.

fun	gun	run	sun
כיף	אקדח	לרוץ	שמש

Name: ____________________ Date: ____________________

Today is: Monday | Tuesday | Wednesday | Thursday | Friday

Direction: Trace and read the sentences.

bag	rag	tag	wag

תיק	סמרטוט	תגית	מתנודד

He has many bags.

I see a rag.

I see a tag.

Its tail is wagging.

My Sight Word List

English - Hebrew

a	in	said
and	is	see
away	it	the
big	jump	three
blue	little	to
can	look	two
come	make	up
down	me	we
find	my	where
for	not	yellow
funny	one	you
go	day	
help	play	
here	red	
I	run	

Name: ____________________ Date: ____________________

Today is: Monday | Tuesday | Wednesday | Thursday | Friday

Direction: Trace and read the sentences.

fun	gun	run	sun
	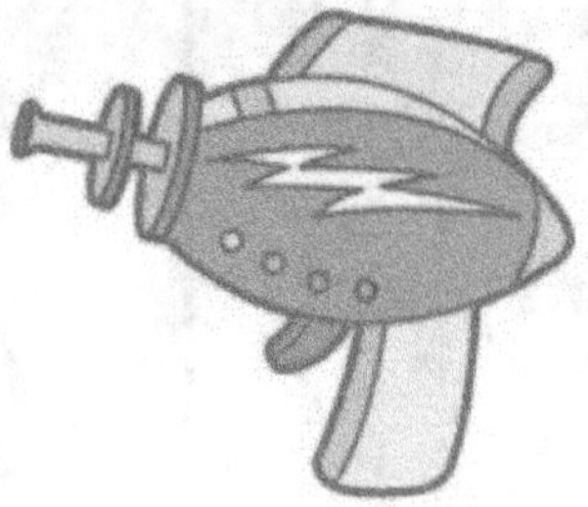		
כיף	אקדח	לרוץ	שמש

They are having fun.

He has a gun.

The bear is running.

The sun is smiling.

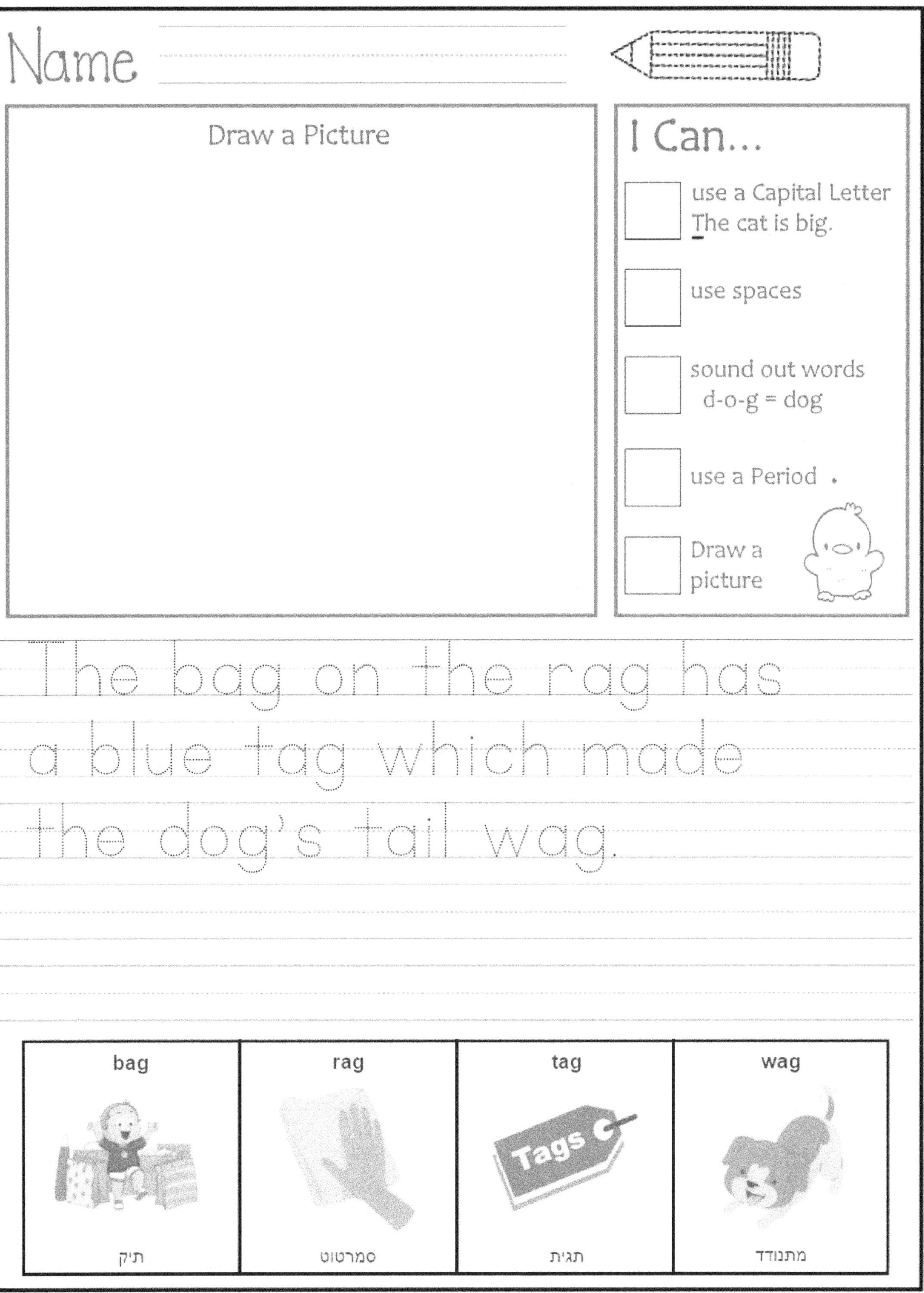

Name

Draw a Picture

I Can...

use a Capital Letter
The cat is big.

use spaces

sound out words
d-o-g = dog

use a Period .

Draw a
picture

The bag on the rag has
a blue tag which made
the dog's tail wag.

bag
תיק

rag
סמרטוט

tag
תגית

wag
מתנודד

Name: ____________________ Date: ____________________

Today is: Monday Tuesday Wednesday Thursday Friday

Direction: Trace and read the sentences.

can	man	pan	van

פחיות	איש	מחבת	ואן

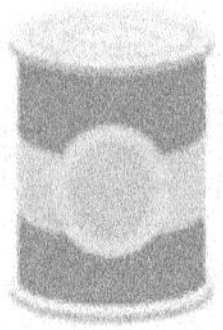

I see a can of soda.

The man is happy.

The pan is dirty.

I see a big van.

Name ______________________

Draw a Picture

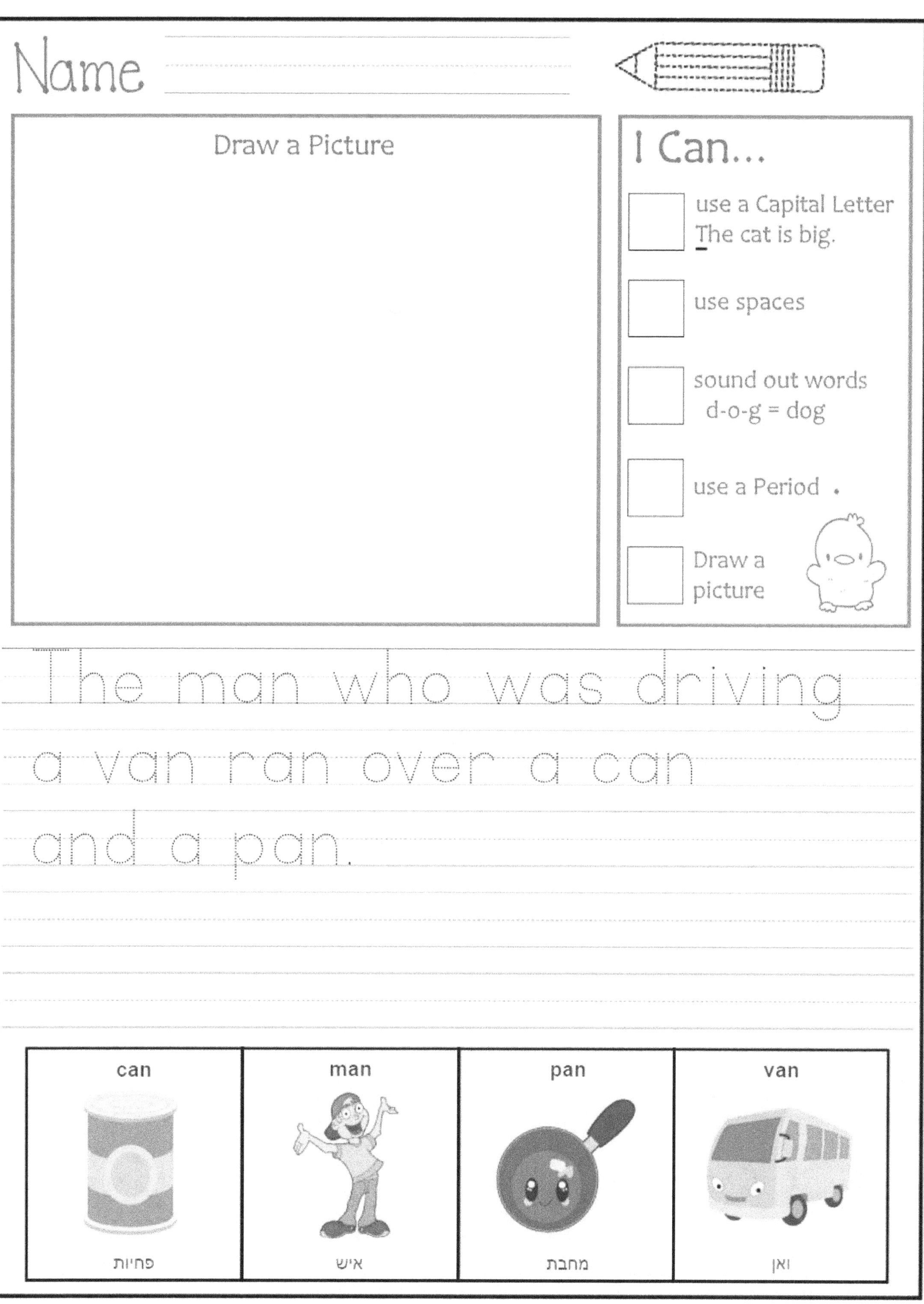

I Can...

- ☐ use a Capital Letter
  <u>T</u>he cat is big.

- ☐ use spaces

- ☐ sound out words
  d-o-g = dog

- ☐ use a Period .

- ☐ Draw a picture

The man who was driving a van ran over a can and a pan.

can	man	pan	van
פחיות	איש	מחבת	וואן

Direction: Trace and read the sentences.

cut	gut	hut	nut
גזירה	בטן	צריף	אגוז

He cut his nails.

He has a gut.

This is a small hut.

It is holding a nut.

Name

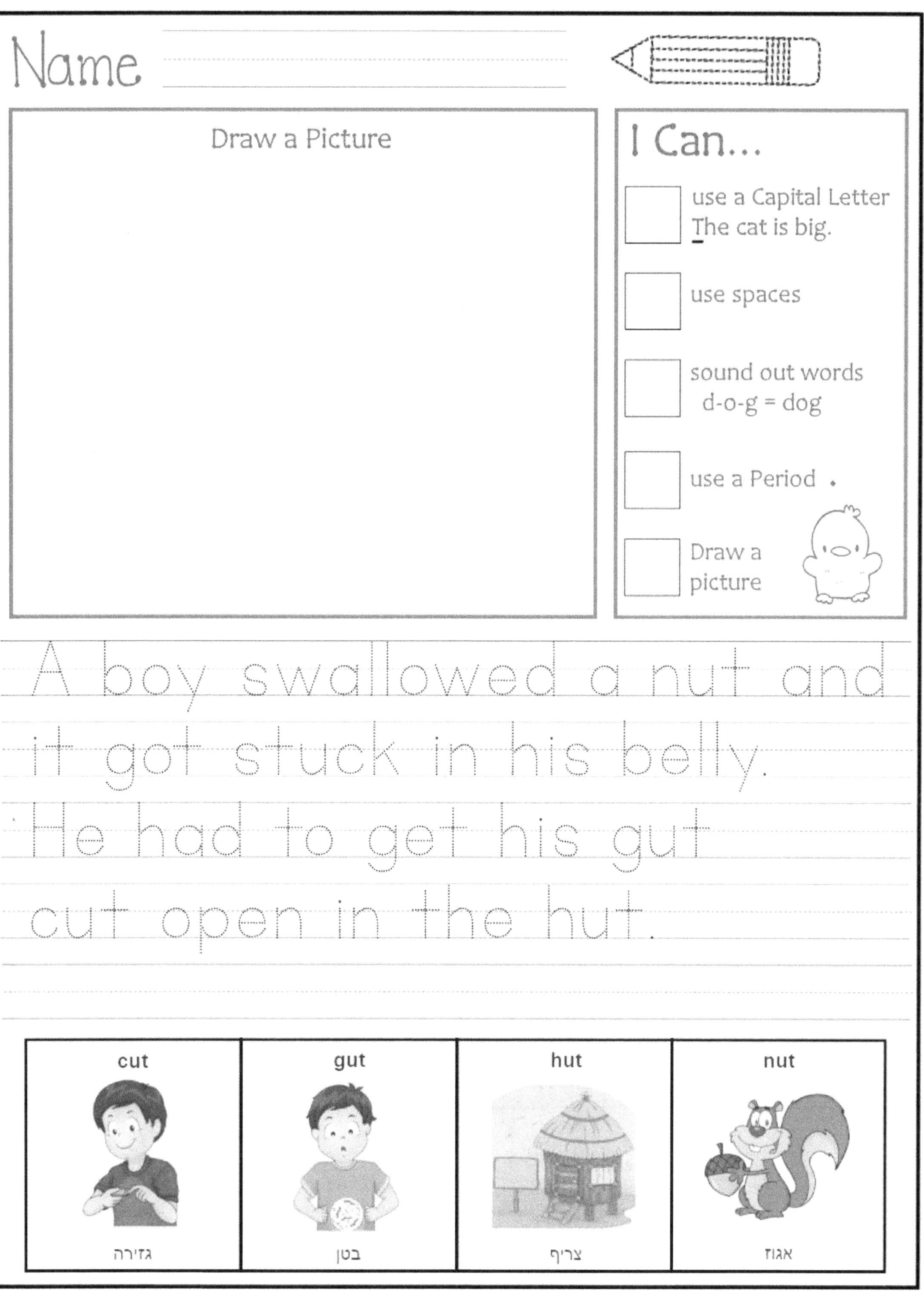
Draw a Picture

I Can...
use a Capital Letter
The cat is big.
use spaces
sound out words
d-o-g = dog
use a Period .
Draw a picture

A boy swallowed a nut and
it got stuck in his belly.
He had to get his gut
cut open in the hut.

cut
גזירה
gut
בטן
hut
צריף
nut
אגוז

Name: ____________________ Date: ____________________

Today is: Monday Tuesday Wednesday Thursday Friday

Direction: Trace and read the sentences.

fat	cat	hat	mat
		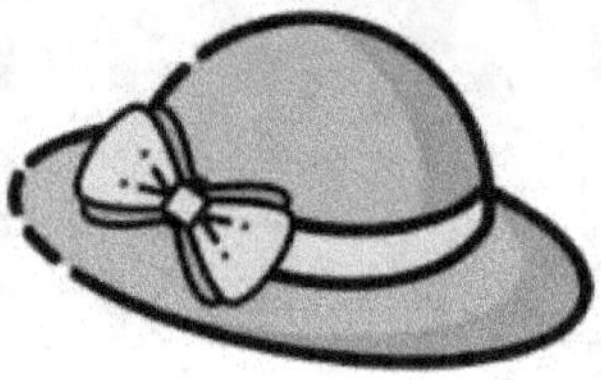	
שמן	חתול	כובע	מחצלת

I see a fat dog.

This is my little cat.

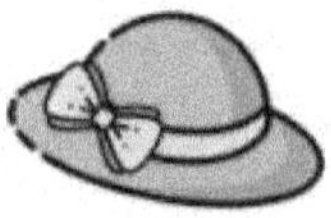

I like this hat.

I see a big mat.

The fat cat laid on the mat that was a hat pattern.

fat	cat	hat	mat
שמן	חתול	כובע	מחצלת

Name: _______________ Date: _______________

Today is: | Monday | Tuesday | Wednesday |
| Thursday | Friday |

Direction: Trace and read the sentences.

cab	lab	tab	crab
מונית	מעבדה	כרטיסייה	סרטן

The cab is fast.

The lab is exciting.

The tab is long.

We found a crab.

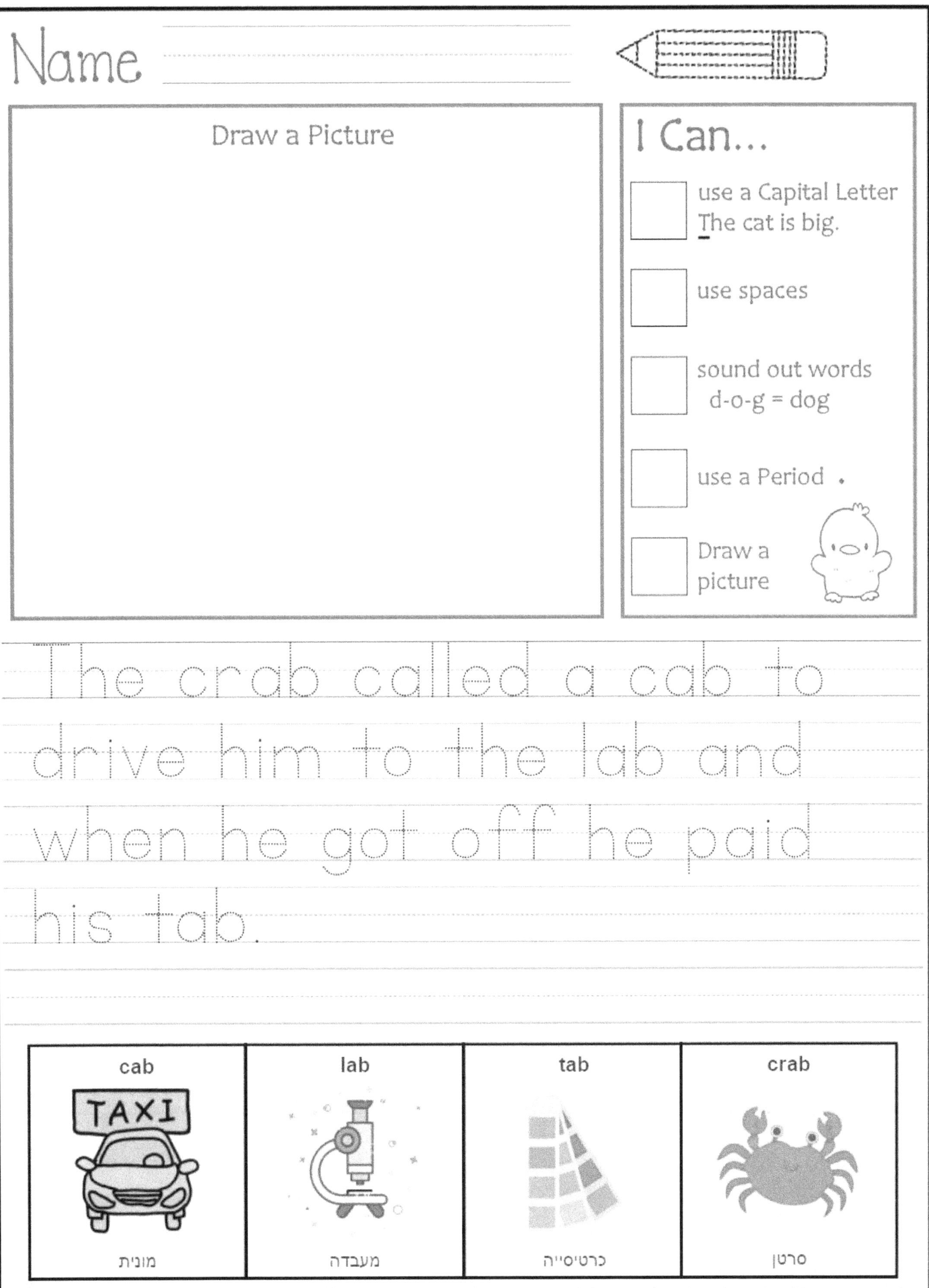

Name
Draw a Picture
I Can...
use a Capital Letter
The cat is big.
use spaces
sound out words
d-o-g = dog
use a Period .
Draw a picture
The crab called a cab to drive him to the lab and when he got off he paid his tab.
cab
TAXI
מונית
lab
מעבדה
tab
כרטיסייה
crab
סרטן

Name: ____________________ Date: ____________________

Today is: Monday | Tuesday | Wednesday | Thursday | Friday

Direction: Trace and read the sentences.

ham	jam	ram	clam

חזיר	ריבה	כבשים	צדף

 I like to eat ham.

 We like to eat jam.

 The ram is big.

 The clam is pretty.

Name

I Can...

☐ use a Capital Letter
_The cat is big.

☐ use spaces

☐ sound out words
d-o-g = dog

☐ use a Period .

☐ Draw a
picture

The clam gave the ram
ham. Then the ram gave
the clam jam.

ham	jam	ram	clam
חזיר	ריבה	כבשים	צדף

Name: ______________ Date: ______________

Today is: Monday Tuesday Wednesday Thursday Friday

Direction: Trace and read the sentences.

bed	led	red	wed

מיטה	מוביל	אדום	חתונה

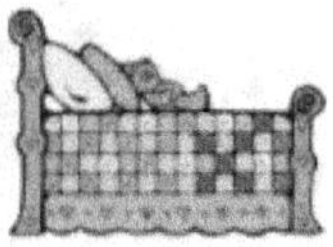 This is my little bed.

 He led us to safety.

 The apple is red.

 He asks her to wed.

When the prince got out of bed, he was led on a red carpet to be wed with the princess.

bed	led	red	wed
מיטה	מוביל	אדום	חתונה

Name: _______________ Date: _______________

Today is: Monday   Tuesday   Wednesday
           Thursday   Friday

Direction: Trace and read the sentences.

bad	dad	mad	sad
רע	אבא	כועס	עצוב

This apple is bad.

My dad is very kind.

The reindeer is mad.

The little cat is sad.

Name _______________________________

Draw a Picture

I Can...

- [ ] use a Capital Letter
  <u>T</u>he cat is big.

- [ ] use spaces

- [ ] sound out words
  d-o-g = dog

- [ ] use a Period .

- [ ] Draw a picture

I was bad so my dad
got mad and now
I am so sad.

bad	dad	mad	sad
רע	אבא	כועס	עצוב

Name: ______________________ Date: ______________________

Today is: Monday Tuesday Wednesday Thursday Friday

Direction: Trace and read the sentences.

den	hen	pen	ten

den	תרנגולת	אורוות	עשר

It is a den.

The hens lay eggs.

She has a good pen.

The ten is smiling.

I Can...

- [ ] use a Capital Letter
  The cat is big.
- [ ] use spaces
- [ ] sound out words
  d-o-g = dog
- [ ] use a Period .
- [ ] Draw a picture

The hen that lived in the
pen laid ten eggs
in her den.

den	hen	pen	ten
den	תרנגולת	אורוות	עשר

Name: ___________________ Date: ___________

Today is: Monday | Tuesday | Wednesday | Thursday | Friday

Direction: Trace and read the sentences.

gum	mum	sum	drum
מסטיק	אמא	סכום	תוף

I like to chew gum.

My mum is kind!

I can do a sum!

The drum is big.

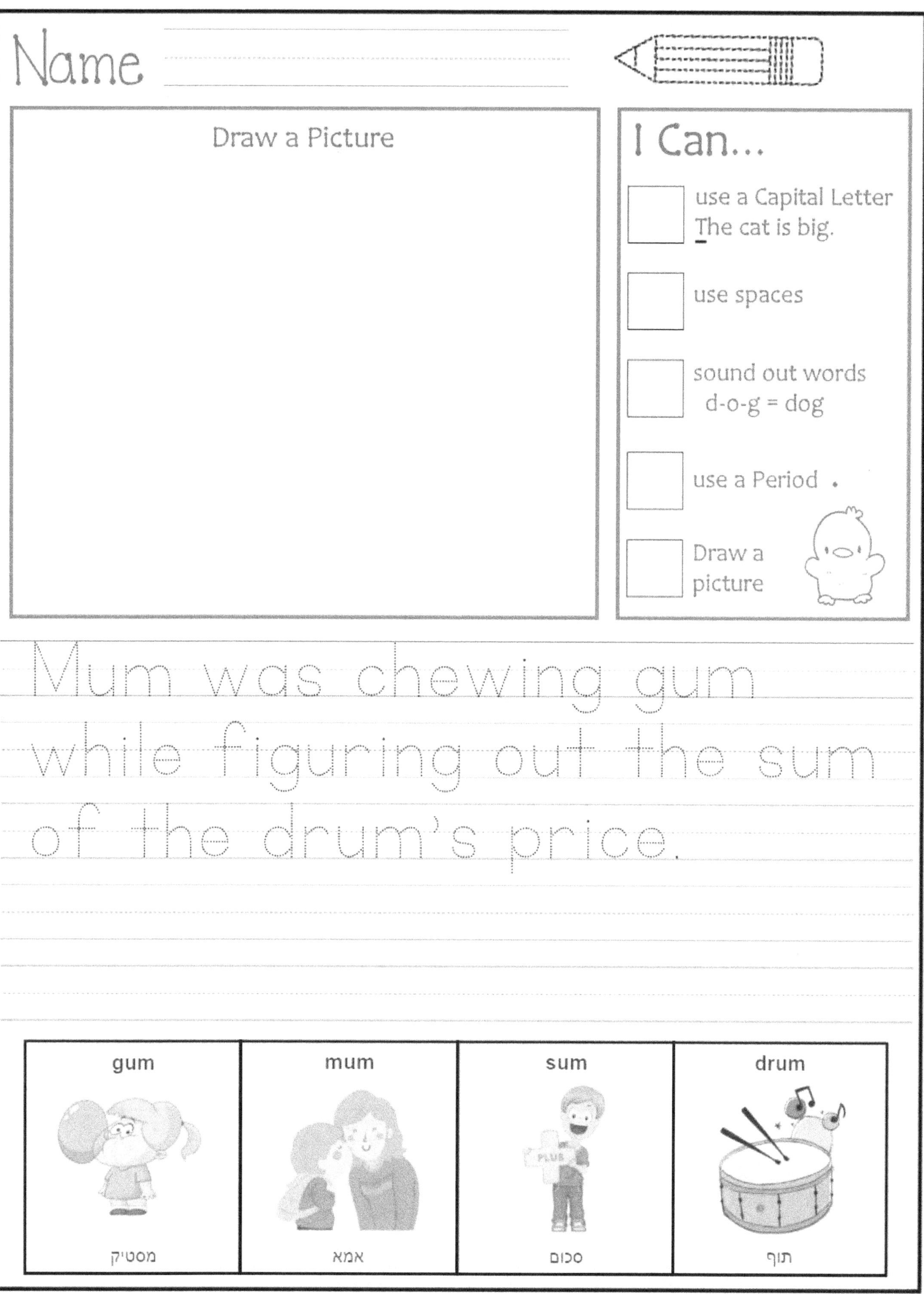

Name

Draw a Picture

I Can...

use a Capital Letter
The cat is big.

use spaces

sound out words
d-o-g = dog

use a Period .

Draw a
picture

Mum was chewing gum
while figuring out the sum
of the drum's price.

gum

mum

sum

drum

מסטיק

אמא

סכום

תוף

Name: _______________ Date: _______________

Today is: Monday Tuesday Wednesday Thursday Friday

Direction: Trace and read the sentences.

bid	hid	kid	lid
הצעת מחיר	להתחבא	ילד	מכסה

He likes to bid.

He is hiding.

The kid like to play.

I see a lid.

Draw a Picture

I Can...

☐ use a Capital Letter
The cat is big.

☐ use spaces

☐ sound out words
d-o-g = dog

☐ use a Period .

☐ Draw a picture

The kid bid a lid for one hundred dollars then hid from his mad parents.

bid	hid	kid	lid
הצעת מחיר	להתחבא	ילד	מכסה

Name: ____________________ Date: ____________________

Today is: Monday Tuesday Wednesday Thursday Friday

Direction: Trace and read the sentences.

big	dig	pig	wig
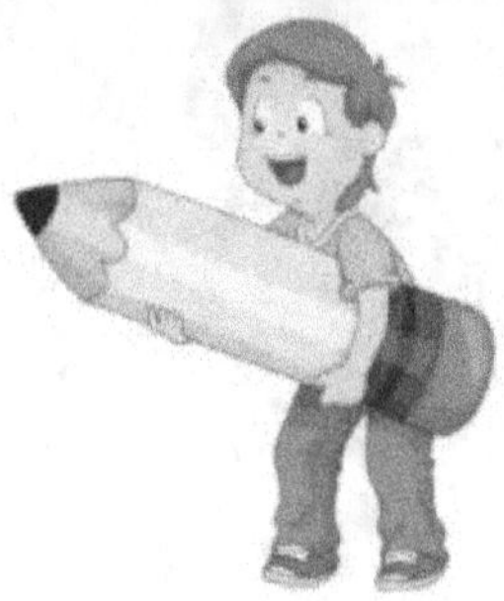	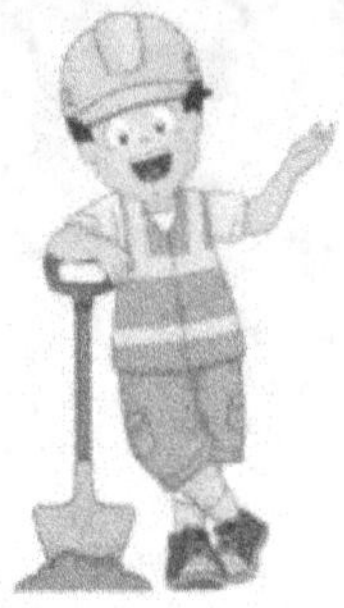	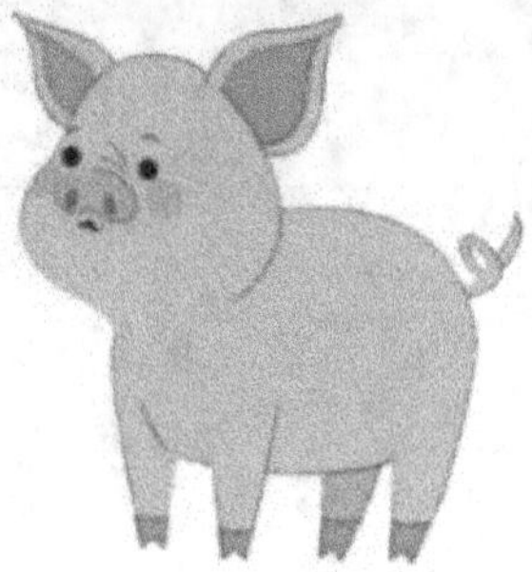	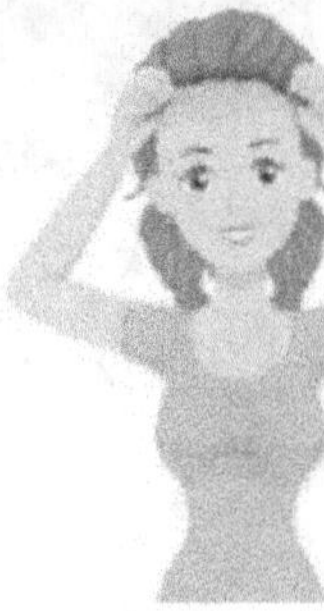
גדול	לחפור	חזיר	פאה

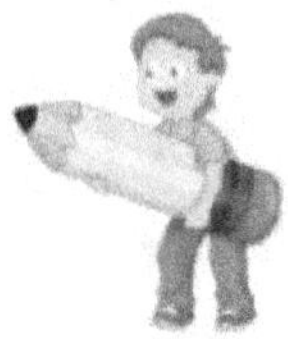

That is a big pencil.

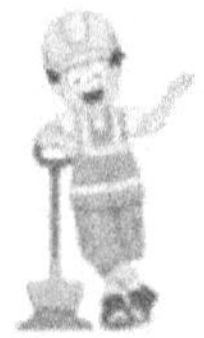

He will dig up a hole.

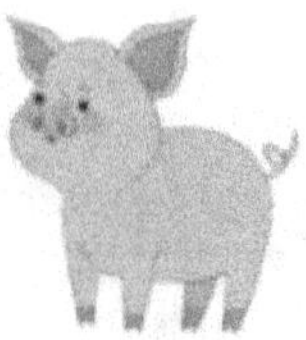

The pig is fat.

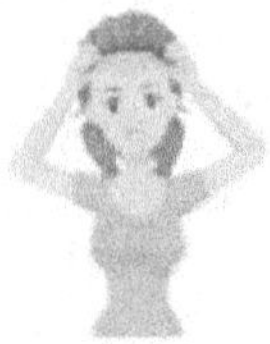

She puts on a wig.

Draw a Picture

I Can...

☐ use a Capital Letter
The cat is big.

☐ use spaces

☐ sound out words
d-o-g = dog

☐ use a Period .

☐ Draw a picture

The big pig went to dig in the mud for his wig.

big	dig	pig	wig
גדול	לחפור	חזיר	פאה

Name: ______________________ Date: ______________________

Today is: Monday Tuesday Wednesday Thursday Friday

Direction: Trace and read the sentences.

bin	fin	pin	win
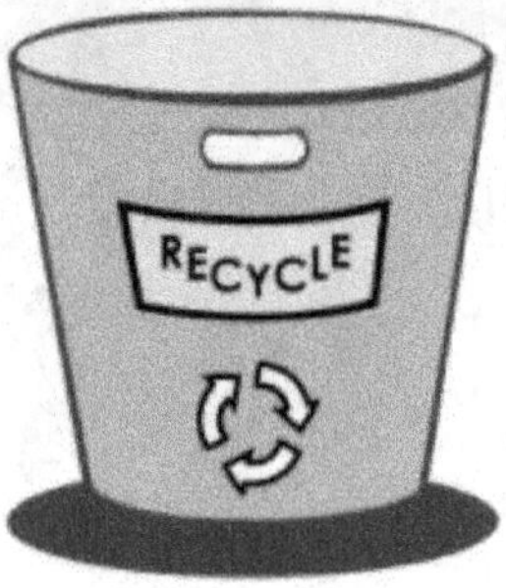	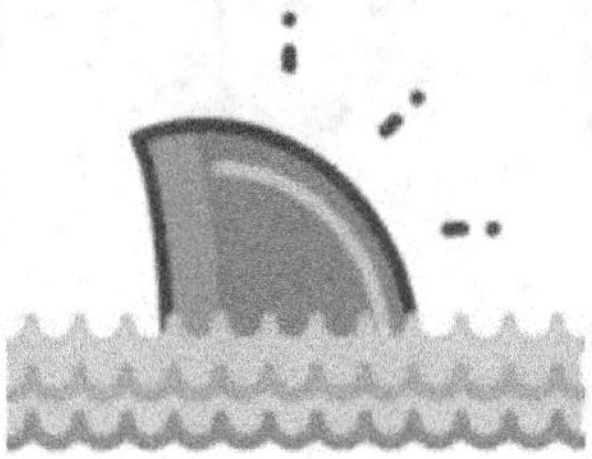	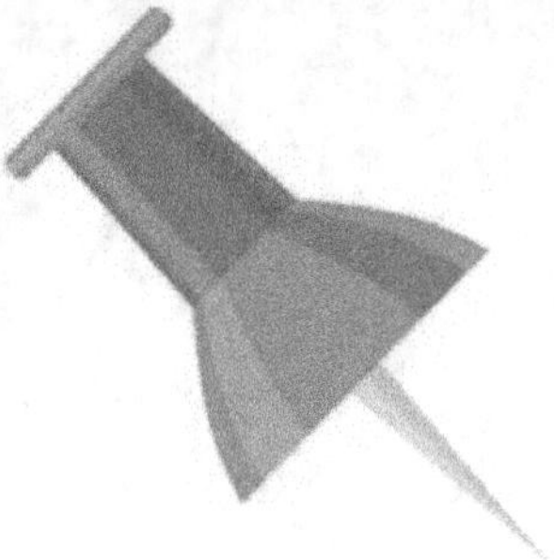	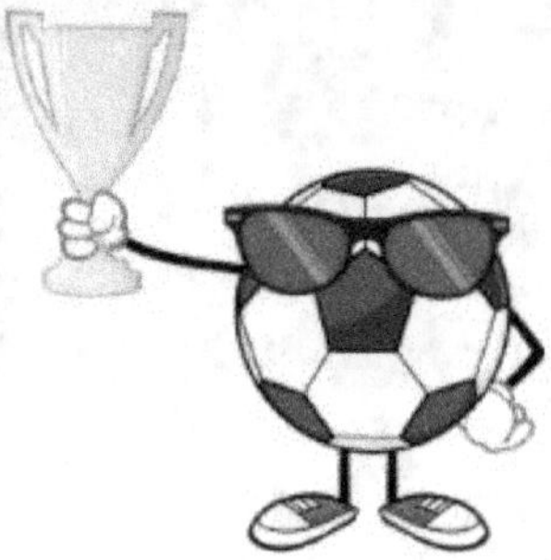
סל	סנפיר	סיכה	לנצח

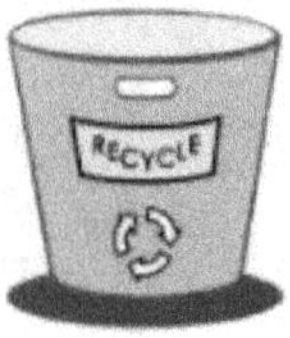

It is a recycle bin.

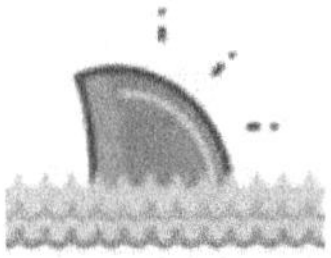

The shark has a fin.

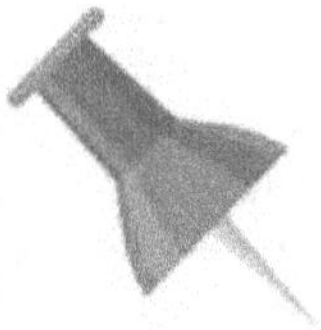

The pin is pointy.

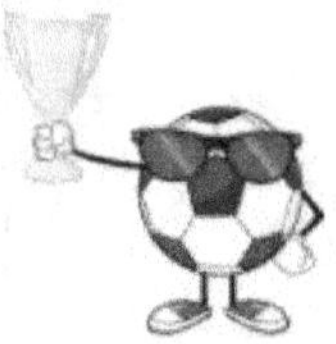

He won the match.

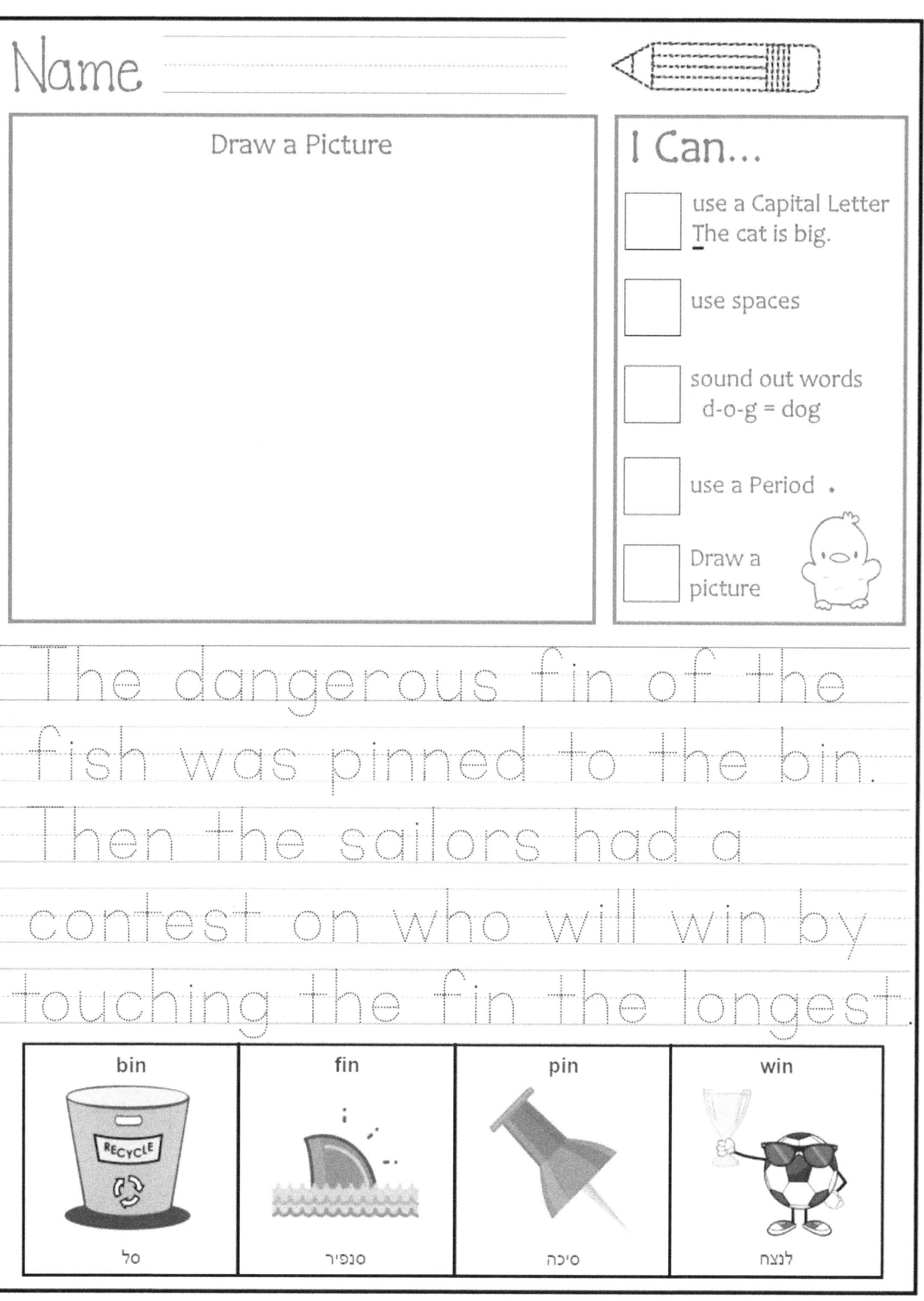

Name
Draw a Picture
I Can...
use a Capital Letter
The cat is big.
use spaces
sound out words
d-o-g = dog
use a Period .
Draw a picture
The dangerous fin of the fish was pinned to the bin. Then the sailors had a contest on who will win by touching the fin the longest.
bin
סל
fin
סנפיר
pin
סיכה
win
לנצח
RECYCLE

Name: ____________________ Date: ____________________

Today is: Monday Tuesday Wednesday Thursday Friday

Direction: Trace and read the sentences.

hip	lip	nip	sip

ירך	שפתיים	צביטה	לשתות

This is my hip.

Her lips are red.

It is nipping its toy.

She is sipping.

Draw a Picture

I Can...

- [ ] use a Capital Letter
  <u>T</u>he cat is big.

- [ ] use spaces

- [ ] sound out words
  d-o-g = dog

- [ ] use a Period .

- [ ] Draw a picture

The dog nipped someone
who was sipping water
with his lip.

hip	lip	nip	sip
ירך	שפתיים	צביטה	לשתות

Name: ____________________ Date: ____________________

Today is: Monday Tuesday Wednesday Thursday Friday

Direction: Trace and read the sentences.

fit	hit	kit	sit
		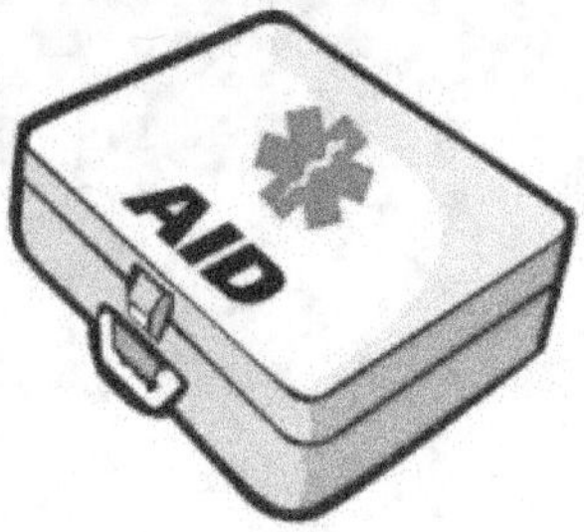	
בכושר	מכה	ערכה	לשבת

It is perfectly fit.

They hit each other.

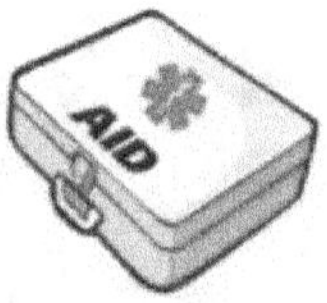

That is a safety kit.

He is sitting.

The fit doctor sat then
was hit by a kit.

fit	hit	kit	sit
בכושר	מכה	ערכה	לשבת

Name: ____________________ Date: ____________________

Today is: Monday Tuesday Wednesday Thursday Friday

Direction: Trace and read the sentences.

cob	job	rob	sob

תירס	עבודה	לשדוד	בוכה

 I ate corn on the cob.

 This is my job.

 He is robbing.

 The girl is sobbing.

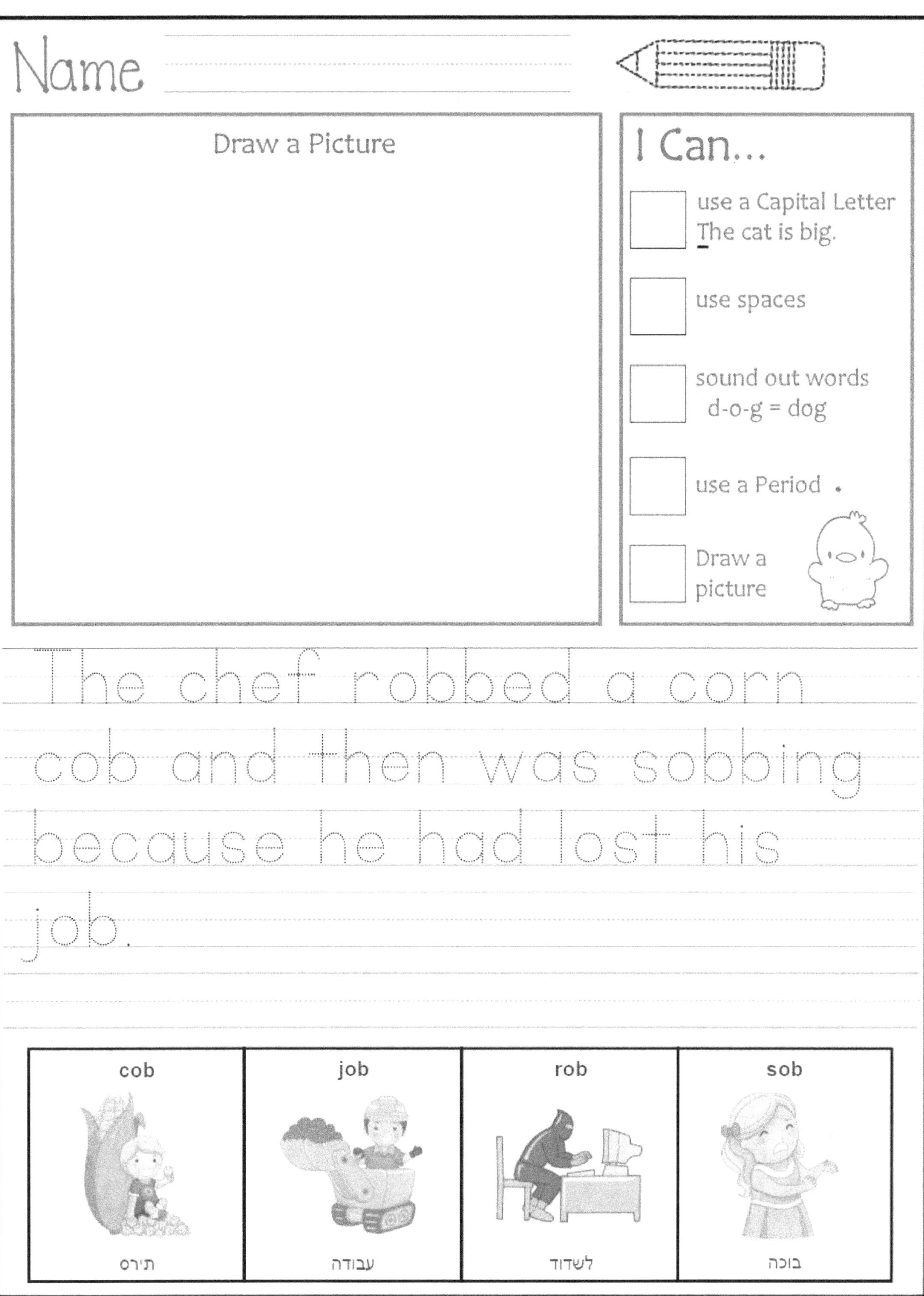

Name

Draw a Picture

I Can...

- [ ] use a Capital Letter
  <u>T</u>he cat is big.
- [ ] use spaces
- [ ] sound out words
  d-o-g = dog
- [ ] use a Period .
- [ ] Draw a picture

The chef robbed a corn cob and then was sobbing because he had lost his job.

cob	job	rob	sob
תירס	עבודה	לשדוד	בוכה

Name: ____________________ Date: ____________________

Today is: Monday | Tuesday | Wednesday | Thursday | Friday

Direction: Trace and read the sentences.

dog	**hog**	**jog**	**log**
			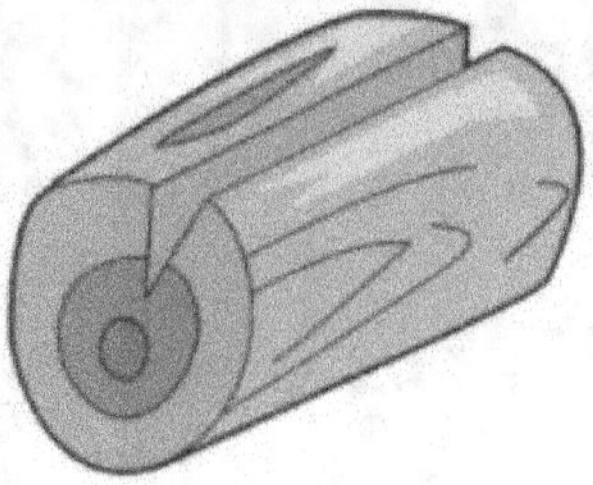
כלב	חזיר	ריצה קלה	עץ

 The dog is thrilled.

 The hog is big.

 She is jogging.

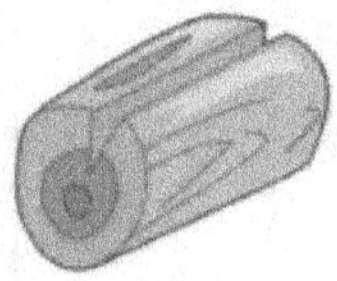 The log is small.

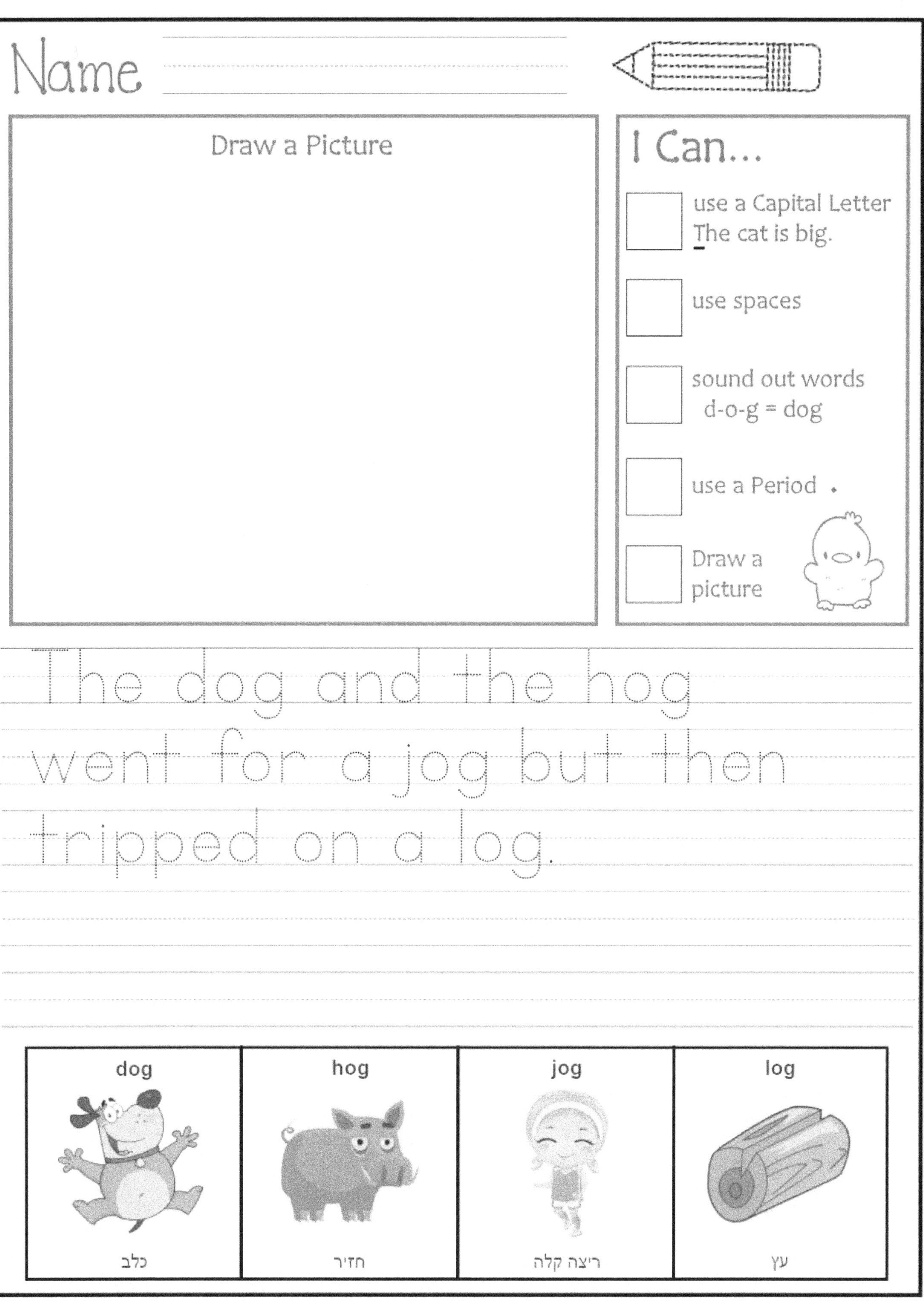

Name

Draw a Picture

I Can...

use a Capital Letter
The cat is big.

use spaces

sound out words
d-o-g = dog

use a Period .

Draw a
picture

The dog and the hog
went for a jog but then
tripped on a log.

dog
כלב

hog
חזיר

jog
ריצה קלה

log
עץ

Name: _______________ Date: _______________

Today is: Monday Tuesday Wednesday Thursday Friday

Direction: Trace and read the sentences.

bug	hug	jug	mug
חרק	חיבוק	כד	ספל

The bug is colorful.

She is hugging.

The jug has milk in it.

He has a mug.

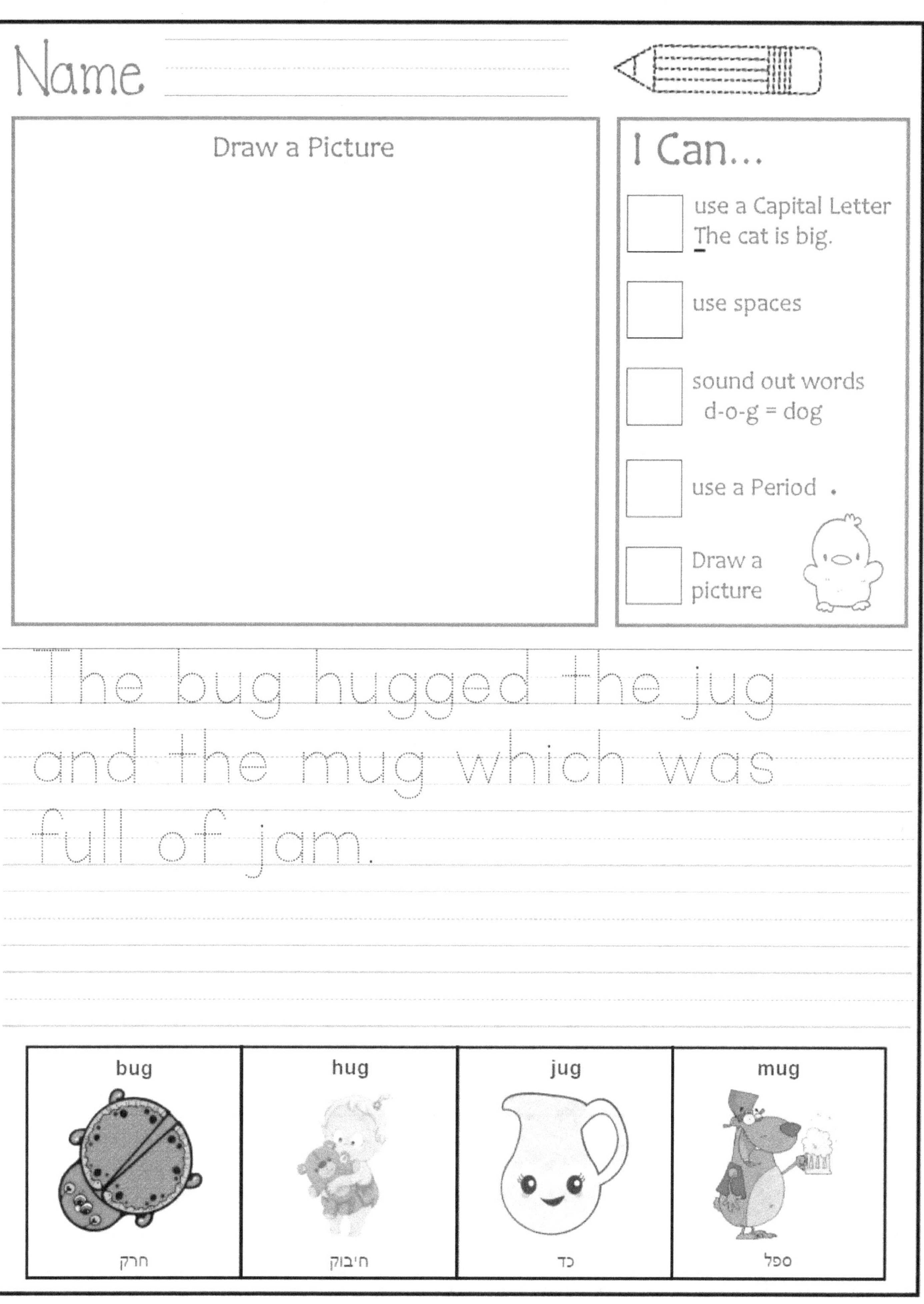

Name

Draw a Picture

I Can...

use a Capital Letter
The cat is big.

use spaces

sound out words
d-o-g = dog

use a Period .

Draw a
picture

The bug hugged the jug
and the mug which was
full of jam.

bug
חרק

hug
חיבוק

jug
כד

mug
ספל

Name: ______________ Date: ______________

Today is: Monday | Tuesday | Wednesday | Thursday | Friday

Direction: Trace and read the sentences.

cot	dot	hot	pot

מיטה	נקודה	חם	סיר

This is my cot.

There are many dots.

It is very hot.

He has a plant pot.

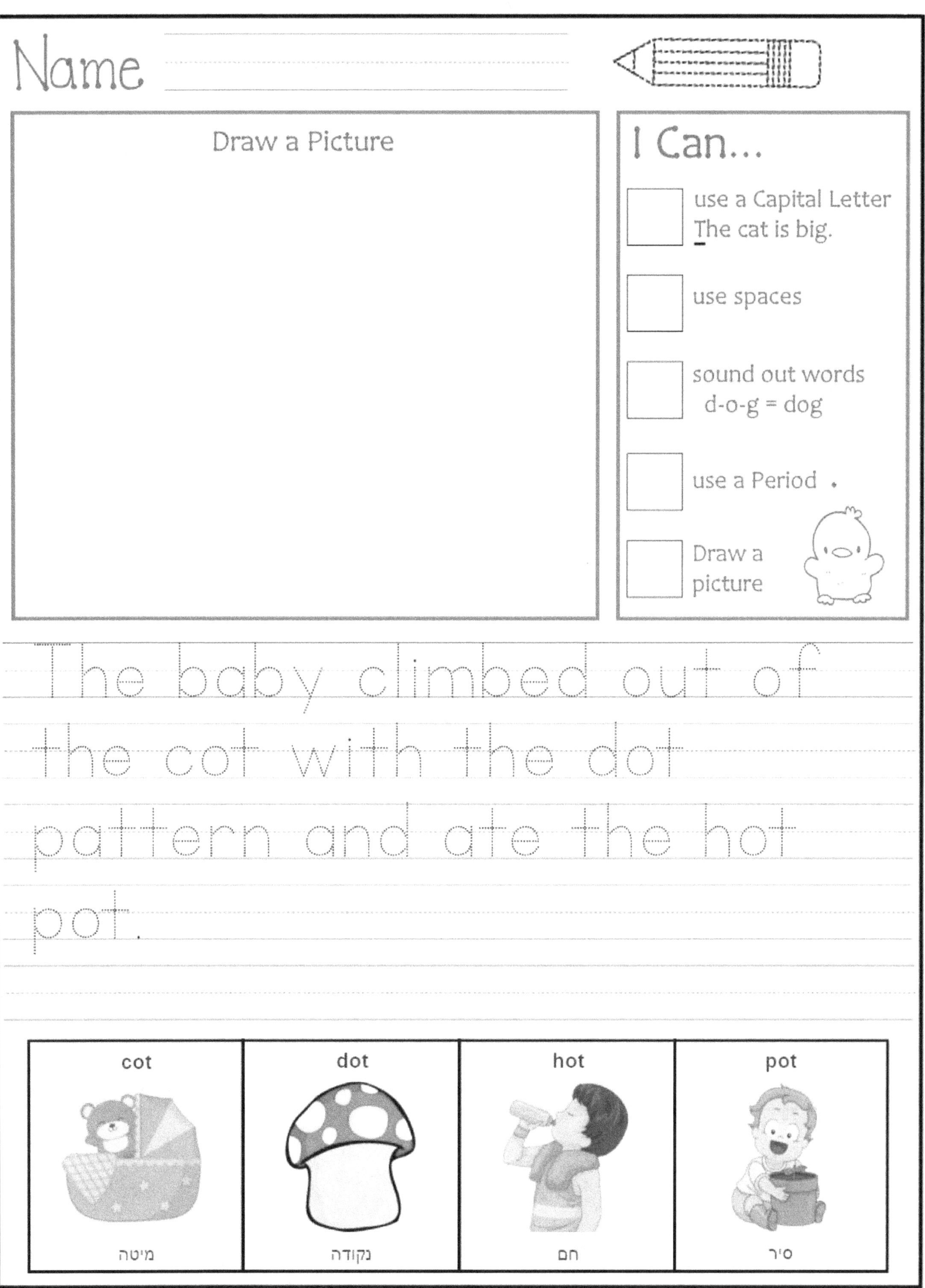

Name

Draw a Picture

I Can...

use a Capital Letter
The cat is big.

use spaces

sound out words
d-o-g = dog

use a Period .

Draw a
picture

The baby climbed out of
the cot with the dot
pattern and ate the hot
pot.

cot
מיטה

dot
נקודה

hot
חם

pot
סיר

Name: _________________________ Date: _________________

Today is: Monday Tuesday Wednesday Thursday Friday

Direction: Read the words and make a sentence.

fun	gun	run	sun
כיף	אקדח	לרוץ	שמש

Name

Draw a Picture

I Can...

- ☐ use a Capital Letter
  <u>T</u>he cat is big.

- ☐ use spaces

- ☐ sound out words
  d-o-g = dog

- ☐ use a Period .

- ☐ Draw a picture

Name: _______________________ Date: _______________

Today is: Monday Tuesday Wednesday
Thursday Friday

Name: _________________________ Date: _________________

Today is: [Monday] [Tuesday] [Wednesday]
[Thursday] [Friday]

Direction: Read the words and make a sentence.

bag	rag	tag	wag
 תיק	 סמרטוט	Tags תגית	 מתנודד

Name

Draw a Picture

I Can...

☐ use a Capital Letter
<u>T</u>he cat is big.

☐ use spaces

☐ sound out words
d-o-g = dog

☐ use a Period .

☐ Draw a picture

Name: _______________________ Date: _______________

Today is: | Monday | Tuesday | Wednesday |
           | Thursday | Friday |

Name: ___________________ Date: ___________

Today is: Monday | Tuesday | Wednesday | Thursday | Friday

Direction: Read the words and make a sentence.

can	man	pan	van
פחיות	איש	מחבת	ואן

Name ___________________________

<table>
<tr><td>

Draw a Picture

</td><td>

I Can...

☐ use a Capital Letter
<u>T</u>he cat is big.

☐ use spaces

☐ sound out words
d-o-g = dog

☐ use a Period .

☐ Draw a
picture

</td></tr>
</table>

Name: _______________________ Date: _______________________

Today is: Monday Tuesday Wednesday Thursday Friday

cut	gut	hut	nut
גזירה	בטן	צריף	אגוז

Name ____________________

Draw a Picture

I Can...

- [ ] use a Capital Letter
  <u>T</u>he cat is big.

- [ ] use spaces

- [ ] sound out words
  d-o-g = dog

- [ ] use a Period .

- [ ] Draw a picture

Name: _____________________ Date: _____________

Today is: Monday Tuesday Wednesday Thursday Friday

Name: _______________________ Date: _______________________

Today is: Monday Tuesday Wednesday
Thursday Friday

Direction: Read the words and make a sentence.

fat	cat	hat	mat
שמן	חתול	כובע	מחצלת

Draw a Picture

I Can...

use a Capital Letter
The cat is big.

use spaces

sound out words
d-o-g = dog

use a Period .

Draw a
picture

Name: _______________________ Date: _______________

Today is: Monday   Tuesday   Wednesday   Thursday   Friday

Name: ___________________ Date: ___________________

Today is: [Monday] [Tuesday] [Wednesday]
[Thursday] [Friday]

Direction: Read the words and make a sentence.

cab	lab	tab	crab
מונית	מעבדה	כרטיסייה	סרטן

Name

Draw a Picture

I Can...

- [ ] use a Capital Letter
  The cat is big.

- [ ] use spaces

- [ ] sound out words
  d-o-g = dog

- [ ] use a Period .

- [ ] Draw a picture

Name: _______________________   Date: _______________

Today is: [Monday] [Tuesday] [Wednesday]
          [Thursday] [Friday]

Name: _________________ Date: _______________

Today is: Monday Tuesday Wednesday Thursday Friday

Direction: Read the words and make a sentence.

ham	jam	ram	clam
חזיר	ריבה	כבשים	צדף

Name

Draw a Picture

I Can...

☐ use a Capital Letter
The cat is big.

☐ use spaces

☐ sound out words
d-o-g = dog

☐ use a Period .

☐ Draw a picture

Name: ___________________   Date: ___________________

Today is: | Monday | Tuesday | Wednesday |
| Thursday | Friday |

Name: _______________________ Date: _______________

Today is: | Monday | Tuesday | Wednesday |
 | Thursday | Friday |

Direction: Read the words and make a sentence.

bed	led	red	wed
מיטה	מוביל	אדום	חתונה

Name

Draw a Picture

I Can...

- [ ] use a Capital Letter
  The cat is big.

- [ ] use spaces

- [ ] sound out words
  d-o-g = dog

- [ ] use a Period .

- [ ] Draw a picture

Name: _______________________ Date: _______________

Today is: Monday Tuesday Wednesday Thursday Friday

Name: _______________ Date: _______________

Today is: [Monday] [Tuesday] [Wednesday]
[Thursday] [Friday]

Direction: Read the words and make a sentence.

bad	dad	mad	sad
רע	אבא	כועס	עצוב

Name _______________________

Draw a Picture

I Can...

- [ ] use a Capital Letter
  <u>T</u>he cat is big.

- [ ] use spaces

- [ ] sound out words
  d-o-g = dog

- [ ] use a Period .

- [ ] Draw a picture

Name: _________________________ Date: _________________________

Today is: Monday Tuesday Wednesday Thursday Friday

Name: _________________________ Date: _________________

Today is: Monday Tuesday Wednesday Thursday Friday

Direction: Read the words and make a sentence.

den	hen	pen	ten

Name

Draw a Picture

I Can...

- [ ] use a Capital Letter
  The cat is big.

- [ ] use spaces

- [ ] sound out words
  d-o-g = dog

- [ ] use a Period .

- [ ] Draw a picture

Name: _______________________ Date: _______________

Today is: Monday Tuesday Wednesday
Thursday Friday

Name: _________________________ Date: _________________

Today is: [Monday] [Tuesday] [Wednesday]
[Thursday] [Friday]

Direction: Read the words and make a sentence.

gum	mum	sum	drum
מסטיק	אמא	סכום	תוף

Name

Draw a Picture

I Can...

use a Capital Letter
The cat is big.

use spaces

sound out words
d-o-g = dog

use a Period .

Draw a
picture

Name: ___________________________ Date: ___________

Today is: Monday Tuesday Wednesday Thursday Friday

Name: _______________________   Date: _______________

Today is: [Monday] [Tuesday] [Wednesday]
           [Thursday] [Friday]

Direction: Read the words and make a sentence.

bid	hid	kid	lid
הצעת מחיר	להתחבא	ילד	מכסה

Name

Draw a Picture

I Can...

- [ ] use a Capital Letter
  <u>T</u>he cat is big.

- [ ] use spaces

- [ ] sound out words
  d-o-g = dog

- [ ] use a Period .

- [ ] Draw a picture

Name: _______________________   Date: _______________

Today is: Monday Tuesday Wednesday Thursday Friday

Name: ____________________ Date: ____________________

Today is: Monday Tuesday Wednesday Thursday Friday

Direction: Read the words and make a sentence.

big	dig	pig	wig

גדול	לחפור	חזיר	פאה

Name

Draw a Picture

I Can...

- [ ] use a Capital Letter
  The cat is big.

- [ ] use spaces

- [ ] sound out words
  d-o-g = dog

- [ ] use a Period .

- [ ] Draw a picture

Name: _____________________ Date: _____________________

Today is: | Monday | Tuesday | Wednesday |
Thursday | Friday |

Name: _________________________ Date: _______________

Today is: [Monday] [Tuesday] [Wednesday]

[Thursday] [Friday]

Direction: Read the words and make a sentence.

bin	fin	pin	win
סל	סנפיר	סיכה	לנצח

Name

Draw a Picture

I Can...

- [ ] use a Capital Letter
  The cat is big.

- [ ] use spaces

- [ ] sound out words
  d-o-g = dog

- [ ] use a Period .

- [ ] Draw a picture

Name: _______________________ Date: _______________

Today is: Monday | Tuesday | Wednesday
Thursday | Friday

Name: ___________________ Date: _______________
Today is: Monday Tuesday Wednesday Thursday Friday
Direction: Read the words and make a sentence.

hip
lip
nip
sip
ירך
שפתיים
צביטה
לשתות
slurp

Name

Draw a Picture

I Can...

- [ ] use a Capital Letter
  The cat is big.

- [ ] use spaces

- [ ] sound out words
  d-o-g = dog

- [ ] use a Period .

- [ ] Draw a picture

Name: _______________________ Date: _______________________

Today is: Monday Tuesday Wednesday Thursday Friday

Name: _______________________ Date: _______________

Today is: Monday | Tuesday | Wednesday
Thursday | Friday

Direction: Read the words and make a sentence.

fit	hit	kit	sit
בכושר	מכה	ערכה	לשבת

Name

Draw a Picture

I Can...

- [ ] use a Capital Letter
  The cat is big.

- [ ] use spaces

- [ ] sound out words
  d-o-g = dog

- [ ] use a Period .

- [ ] Draw a picture

Name: ______________________   Date: ______________

Today is: Monday   Tuesday   Wednesday   Thursday   Friday

Name: _______________________ Date: _______________________

Today is: Monday   Tuesday   Wednesday   Thursday   Friday

Direction: Read the words and make a sentence.

cob	job	rob	sob
תירס	עבודה	לשדוד	בוכה

Name ___________

Draw a Picture

I Can...

- ☐ use a Capital Letter
  <u>T</u>he cat is big.

- ☐ use spaces

- ☐ sound out words
  d-o-g = dog

- ☐ use a Period .

- ☐ Draw a picture

Name: _______________ Date: _______________

Today is: Monday Tuesday Wednesday
Thursday Friday

Name: _________________ Date: _______________

Today is: Monday Tuesday Wednesday
Thursday Friday

Direction: Read the words and make a sentence.

dog	hog	jog	log
כלב	חזיר	ריצה קלה	עץ

____

____

____

____

____

Name _______________________

<table>
<tr><td>Draw a Picture</td><td>I Can...</td></tr>
</table>

Draw a Picture

I Can...

☐ use a Capital Letter
The cat is big.

☐ use spaces

☐ sound out words
d-o-g = dog

☐ use a Period .

☐ Draw a picture

Name: _______________________ Date: _______________

Today is:
Monday Tuesday Wednesday
Thursday Friday

Name: _______________________ Date: _______________

Today is: Monday Tuesday Wednesday Thursday Friday

Direction: Read the words and make a sentence.

bug	**hug**	**jug**	**mug**
חרק	חיבוק	כד	ספל

Name

<table>
<tr><td>Draw a Picture</td><td>

I Can...

☐ use a Capital Letter
The cat is big.

☐ use spaces

☐ sound out words
d-o-g = dog

☐ use a Period .

☐ Draw a picture

</td></tr>
</table>

Name: _________________________ Date: _________________

Today is: [Monday] [Tuesday] [Wednesday] [Thursday] [Friday]

Name: _________________ Date: _________________

Today is: Monday Tuesday Wednesday Thursday Friday

Direction: Read the words and make a sentence.

cot	dot	hot	pot
מיטה	נקודה	חם	סיר

Name

Draw a Picture

I Can...

- [ ] use a Capital Letter
  <u>T</u>he cat is big.

- [ ] use spaces

- [ ] sound out words
  d-o-g = dog

- [ ] use a Period .

- [ ] Draw a picture

Name: _______________________ Date: _______________

Today is: Monday Tuesday Wednesday Thursday Friday

www.ingramcontent.com/pod-product-compliance
Lightning Source LLC
Chambersburg PA
CBHW081351160726
48000CB00010B/3303